Armour

Dedication

Here you go, my granny, as promised.
You have been my constant, my friend, and my conscience.
I love you!

Copyright © 2016 by CHRISTINA R. WILLIAMS.

Library of Congress Control Number:		2016937704
ISBN:	Softcover	978-0-9970364-9-7
	eBook	978-0-9974751-0-4

All rights reserved. No part of this book may be reproduced or transmitted in any form or by any means, electronic or mechanical, including photocopying, recording, or by any information storage and retrieval system, without permission in writing form the copyright owner.

This is a work of fiction and / or personal feelings. Names, characters, places, and incidents either are the products of the author's imagination or are used fictionally, and any resemblance to any actual persons, living or dead, events, or locales is entirely coincidental.

To order additional copies of this book, contact publisher:
Superi LLC.
www.superillc.com

Armour

Table of Contents

Introduction 1
To Give God the Glory 3
Can You Imagine 4
Herald 5
Try and Find 6
Dust Covered Truth 7
Jesus Lives 8
My Testimony 10
My Doubts/His Answers 11
The Road to Salvation 12
The Dream of Reality 14
Rage 16
The Devil's Seed 18
Wayward Soul 19
Crying out 20
Come Back Lord 22
Guardian Grandma 24
Behold the Weeds 26

Salvation Found	27
Battle Lines	28
Joy	30
Christ Calls	32
Daily Toil	34
Remember	36
I'm Sending Out This Letter	38
Opportunity Knocks	40
Look Up All His People	41
The Day Our Savior Died	42
Let the Holy Ghost Come Down	44
No One Like My Lord	46
Sunday Christians	48
Upon a Hill	50
Liars Made	51
As Her Mother	54
Where the World Ends	55
The Ocean Rolls	56
Conclusion	57

Armour

Introduction

I am fallible. My flaws are many. I have been called a sinner and a saint. I've claimed salvation only to slide away. I've returned and reclaimed that first love and first works time and again. I take comfort in knowing that God does not ask for perfection. He seeks only a willing and open spirit and a repentant heart. I am a work in progress.

To Give God the Glory

Thank you, dear Lord, for the blessings that you have bestowed
upon us this day.
For leading, guiding, and directing us in your merciful and caring
way.

We worship you, Lord, for showing us compassion, and teaching
us with a strong hand.
For planting our feet on a righteous path through this worldly and
sinful land.

We praise you, oh God, for your wisdom, and for all the ways you
say,
I'll never leave you, nor forsake you. Father teach us to obey.

We shall keep our eyes eastward bound searching for a sign,
That you have sent your son, at last, so in Heaven we can reside.

Thank you, dear Lord, for sending us a Savior to take away our
sins.
We glorify your wonderful name on earth and in Heaven.

Amen

Can You Imagine

Can you imagine what it took,
For Christ to leave His Father's side,
To be born of flesh a helpless babe,
To choose on Earth to reside?

Can you imagine what it was like,
For a flesh robed God, like He,
To walk among us mortal men,
Knowing what His end would be?

Can you imagine what He must have felt,
Overwhelmed with our sin,
As He braved the world's wrath,
To save the souls of men?

Can you imagine the pain He endured,
A living sacrifice of truth,
As in His mercy from the cross He cried,
"Forgive them. They know not what they do."

Herald

Long ago in a foreign land,
A babe was born in Bethlehem.

Born of flesh, God's holy word,
Entered the world to be heard.

Like the rainbow, a symbol sent,
Of God's faithful love, a testament.

Righteousness personified,
We saw through blinded eyes.

Clouded over by our sin,
And so we crucified Him.

The last breath to escape,
Was spent to forgive our mistake.

From the cross He did cry,
Though yet in sin, they are mine.

He endured the pain,
He bore the shame.

Upon the cross He died,
Within the grave He came alive.

His flesh renewed,
He revealed the good news.

That beyond the grave,
Immortality awaits.

Try and Find

Jesus said "Look, and try to find
Without saying a word, those who are mine."

I searched all the highways and the byways too,
I searched high and low, but wouldn't you know
I found precious few.

Jesus said "Look and try to find
Without saying a word, those who are mine."

I went to the churches, thinking surely they're here,
But when service was o're, and they hit the door,
My eyes filled with tears.

Jesus said "Look and try and find
Without saying a word, those who are mine."

I cried Lord forgive me, for I have failed in this,
Wordless I cannot see, but surely some believe,
Your people are remiss.

And Christ replied, "This is how it will be,
Before the Son of God, comes back for thee."

Dust Covered Truth

Often we say how the times have changed.
Words said from the dawn of time.
Since first one brother turned against another,
Since war did first ignite.

We look to yesterday in search of tomorrow,
Our steps hindered by uncertainty.
We long and wish for days gone by,
Ignoring our current reality.

Swaddled in a world of malicious intent,
We seek a purity we cannot find.
The source buried in morality's grave,
And the travesties leave us blind.

The truth is hidden beneath the lies of man,
Beneath the dust covered Word,
That sits in abject disregard,
Its pages un-cracked and unturned.

It's really a wonder we ponder why life is so hard,
When we've abandoned its very reason.
Ignorance will be a comfortless truth,
That will leave you bereft in its season.

Jesus Lives

He came as a babe to dwell with us.
Lord of lords, His heart was just.

He became a child, His father's son,
And soon thereafter His walk begun.

He went throughout the countryside,
His father's truths He cried.

To save the souls lost in sin,
To heal the hurts of men.

There were those who sought His life,
They filled His days with strife.

They rebuked His words as heresy,
And to the people bellowed, "No mercy."

They resented the lessons He did teach.
They feared the message He did preach.

Until at last He was handed a cross,
And upon Calvary His life was lost

His flesh was torn, His blood spilled,
But His spirit could not be killed.

Wrapped in linen He entered the grave,
But did rise again on that third day.

Everlasting, immortal made,
And now on earth we await.

*The triumphant return of our King.
To join Him in eternity.*

My Testimony

As a young girl I thought I was grown.
I told everyone my life was my own.
I made all the wrong decisions; chose all the wrong paths.
I knew of our Lord, but feared not His wrath.

When I was a teen, I gave my heart to God,
But turned my back when things got hard.

I deceived myself, saying my youth bought me time,
To taste forbidden fruit and to repent of the crime.

I was a sinner, and I married the same,
And we were lost in worldly games.

Of a sudden, like a villain, sorrow's hands did touch,
No words could sooth, the grief too much.

Rock bottom rushed up and swallowed me whole,
I stood on the wire and gambled my soul.

I shook my fist in the face of God,
Blaming Him for this road I'd trod.

In His mercy, by His grace, He did not strike me down,
But taught as a father, of sin's way of coming round.

He spoke of repentance and rebirth,
Of renewal and charity's worth.

By the blood of the Lamb my salvation I claimed,
All praise be to His glorious name.

My Doubts/His Answers

Where is the strength, Lord, you said I would find?
Where is the peace that would calm my troubled mind?

Just look inside your heart, child, for there you will see,
The answers that you seek, you'll find, for there you'll find me.

Lord, life is so very hard. Oh, I don't mean to complain,
But the thoughts I carry deep inside, Lord, I'm so ashamed.

Bring to me your burden's child. I will carry you through.
Ask me for forgiveness. It's waiting right here for you.

Lord, what if I should stumble; what if I should fall?
If I falter, Lord, will I lose it all?

I am a God of mercy, child. Compassion is my name.
Yesterday, and tomorrow, I'm always the same.

The Road to Salvation

I made a bet with a friend of mine,
About a week or two ago,
That her fascination with church would pass,
And if not, I'd with her go,
Though firmly stating only once,
For no faith did I possess,
In things I could not see,
In things I could not test.

I laughed at her naivety,
When first she did confess,
"I found salvation tonight," she cried.
"Oh, good," I mocked, "now let me rest."
I grew angry at her self-righteous claims,
As if a god would even care,
About lowly beings such as us,
Who was she to dare?

Days did pass and weeks did follow,
A fierce rage within broke free.
Where was my friend? Where had she gone?
Why had she abandoned me?
How could she now recall our bet,
And seek the fulfilment of it,
When she knew well the resentment I felt?
Why could she not simply quit?

In a borrowed dress and borrowed heels,
I hid on the far back pew,
Embarrassed for those gathered round,
As I waited for the sermon to conclude.
When chill bumps danced upon my skin,
I thought, this place leaves me cold.
No sooner had the moment passed,
When Christ, to me, made himself known.

My sinful nature was then exposed,
Laid bare before His eyes.
The guilt pressed in, I could not breathe,
I was trapped within my lies.
Tears I wept for my soul's sake,
But it was His blood that washed me clean.
Though my friend found Him first,
We have both been redeemed.

The Dream of Reality

I remember not the slumber,
That slipped me into dream,
But I recall the fear I felt,
As my soul loosed its screams.

The trumpet's blare had sounded,
By the angel of the Lord,
Time for the reaping had come,
With Heaven of one accord.

Left alone in wretched darkness,
My sins I did contemplate,
Yet my remorse and repentance,
Came; in hour, too late.

I'd never doubted who Christ was,
Nor had I believed in another,
But in truth I'd given little thought,
To the hereafter and its wonders.

Yet with hell's gates awaiting me,
I surely wondered now,
And despaired with heavy heart,
That I did not sooner give my vow.

Imprisoned in perpetual night,
I cried futile tears of regret,
And plead ineffectual prayers,
Filled with words I should have said.

Illumination chased the shadows,
To the far corners of my doom,
When an image stood before me,
In my mind, in my room.

He raised me to my feet,
He whispered in my ear,
I offer you my gift of time,
I release you from your fear.

I woke from my troubled slumber,
Sweat slicked and trembling,
With eyes wide open,
I realized it had been a dream.

Pleading for mercy given by grace,
I entrusted my soul to His care,
I repented of my sins,
And now daily for His coming prepare.

Rage

There are people who go to church each Sunday,
They straddle the fence and keep saying one day…

"One day, dear Lord, I'll live only for you,
But the world has a hold on my life too."

And Christ waits patiently for that day to come,
When He can cleanse your sin and say 'welcome home.'

His tears fall from Heaven, as He weeps in sorrow,
An eternity spent waiting for our tomorrow.

"One day, dear Lord, I'll give this world up,
One day I will let you fill my soul's cup."

One day leads to weeks, and weeks into years,
Then comes the rapture, and through tribulation, your tears.

You cry, "Lord, I'm ready to give to you my heart,
I'm ready," you say at last, "a different life to start."

The sky begins to darken from God's released rage,
As a booming voice warns that Satan is freed from his cage.

Then the voice begins to speak, like a rolling thunder in the wind,
"Now every tongue shall confess and every knee shall bend.

I delivered my only Son to bare the weight of the cross,
So salvation could be attained by the lost.

And now you weep, when you find my Son has spoken true?
Depart from me, for you are one I never knew."

Time is not our friend and judgment draws quickly nigh.
Let not your soul perish because you bought the lie.

The Devil's Seed

Prepare, I pray thee, for the words herein,
For upon toes I intend to tread,
Though I do so with a loving heart,
With the Word of God in my head.

They say the road that leads to fire,
Is wide and smoothly paved,
I bid you follow the straighter road,
For at its end you will be saved.

The way of sin sidetracks your path,
With trickery of lust and greed,
Do not be fooled by Satan's plan,
Such are the devil's seeds.

The pleasures of this world are tempting,
I've been lured away myself,
But inside such dens of inequity,
We bring damnation upon ourselves.

The highs this life does offer,
Numb moments we mistake as peace,
What will happen when you wake to realize,
Your salvation has been fleeced?

Wayward Soul

Help me,
For I am too weak to stand.
I'm alone,
In this hostile, bitter land.
I'm trying,
But temptation is strong.
Please, Lord,
Or I won't last for long.

Your compassion,
It's your guidance I seek.
This world,
Is not for the timid or meek.
Find it,
In your heart to forgive me,
I implore,
Though my mistakes are many.

My salvation,
Through you alone waits.
I fear,
Damnation is my fate.
Come now,
I pray, wash me clean.
This sinner,
To unworthily redeem.

Crying out

The smiles and happy laughter,
Are mostly just for show.
The physical pain in my body,
I don't want the world to know.

Inside my heart is breaking,
I cannot help but cry.
The sadness is overpowering,
I seek not pity for the sake of pride.

I struggle with all that's in me,
But my way I still can't find.
There are times when I question,
"Am I losing my mind?"

This road is getting harder,
An uphill battle all the way.
The trials keep on coming,
Getting worse day by day.

I feel like giving up,
No one understands the pain.
I close my eyes, and bow my head,
Oh, Lord, I'm so ashamed.

Some say I should get over it,
Play the hand that I was given.
Some say my sanity,
Lies through the gates of Heaven.

So I cry out to the Lord,
"I need your helping hand.
I'm falling all to pieces, God,
I need your help to stand.

Though in years I am young,
This shell I wear is old.
There is no cure for this body,
So I seek the health of my soul.

At your feet I lay my burdens,
For they are too heavy to bear.
My sorrows I give to thee,
I cast upon you my cares.

Plant my feet on solid ground,
Release me from this pain.
If not that of my body, Lord,
Then of that which causes my shame.

Too often I have turned from you,
When I should have prayed instead.
So fearful of the physical pain,
I left my soul for dead.

So hear this simple plea,
That falls on your holy ears.
Lord, comfort me,
Dry this torrent of tears."

Come Back, Lord

What has happened to me, Jesus?
I can barely hear your call.
I don't know how it happened.
I don't know much at all.
One minute all is fine,
And I'm walking that straight line.
And the next thing I know...
I've gotten into a bind.

I can't find my way back.
I just can't find my way.
Oh Lord, Jesus, come and get me.
Please don't delay.
I need you with me now.
Forgive my sinful doubt.
Renew my spirit, my Lord, I pray.
Hear my desperate shout.

Rekindle the fire,
First set in my soul,
That offered me warmth,
In a world bitter cold.
I know I've gone astray,
And at times games I've played,
But I beg of you, Lord,
Show mercy anyway.

Let your presence be,
A constant where I am.
Take, I pray thee,
Of my seeking hand.
Let my tears of remorse,
Reset my wayward course.
By your blood, wash me clean,
For of purity you are the source.

Guardian Grandma

I said, "God, send down and angel to watch over me,
To show me the right path and there plant my feet.

I turned away from you, and I know that I've done wrong,
Since I made that choice my path has been so very long."

I said, "God, send down an angel to be my guide,
To act as my conscience, and stay by my side."

I said, "Lord, I'm not perfect, and you know all my sins,
But you have the power to see the heart within,

And if when you do, you see a glimmer of hope,
God, send me an angel to be my life's rope,

To help pull me out of this valley I'm in.
God, I need lifted out of this world of sin."

He said, "Child, look beside you, and tell me what you see."
On my left I saw nothing, and on my right, my granny.

He said, "Is she there through thick and through thin?
Is she there through the heartache? Does she look past the sin?"

I said, "Oh yes, Lord. She's my conscience and my guide.
She makes the straight and narrow path seem wide."

"And when you're in the Valley," He asked, "what does she do?"
I said, "She sends down a rope, and helps pull me through."

*He said, "I can forgive the sin, and I'll never leave your side.
But the angel you have asked for, well, on earth she resides."*

Behold the Weeds

The shadow grows long and time still runs eternal.
Perished rose... your lost beauty astounds.

But behold the weeds.

The Ancient oaks hold their ground.
But the saplings flounder mightily.
Saints grow weary.
And the babes are ill-equipped.

But behold the weeds.

The shadow stands frozen as time ceases to exist.
Resurrected roses found thriving beside the sun.

But behold the weeds.

The ancient oaks cannot be found.
And the saplings are left alone.
To fight the weeds to the sun.
As had the roses already home.

The shadow is no more and time means nothing.
Ancient Rose... your power astounds.

Behold... the garden of roses.

Salvation Found

The word of God proclaims that we,
Enter the world robed in flesh and sin.
And that to overcome the world,
We must first be born again.

He did not leave us without hope,
He sent His only Son,
And so began the sacrifice,
To see the will of the Father done.

He never wavered from His course,
As the price of your sin was paid,
His blood upon the cross, the cost,
His life the payment made.

A crown of thorns upon His head,
A spear thrust through His side,
A whip that tore into His flesh,
Upon the cross, Christ died.

Having overcome the sting of death,
Victory is now His crown,
And by the blood He did so shed,
Is our salvation found.

Battle Lines

Good versus evil has come in full sight.

Blessed are they who know wrong from right.

Stay in the light, for midnight has come.

All will be well when the battle is done.

For Satan is sinister, while Christ is kind.

Christians rejoice, and woe, to sinners cry.

For those that can hear the trumpet will blast.

Listen carefully, God's people, for it'll happen fast.

As we speak, Satan is rallying his demons below,

And Christ watches His Father for His cue to go.

The lines have been drawn, and all is in place.

Now is the time to stay strong in your faith.

Now is the hour. Now is the time.

Hallelujah, sweet Jesus, our redemption draws neigh.

The Old Man

Since the days of my careless youth,
I've traveled far from home,
But I remember the blind man,
Who often the streets did roam.

A servant's heart within his chest,
A ready smile to greet,
Upon his tongue words of charity,
Never a stranger to meet.

He had no family to call his own,
None, his blood, who shared,
The body of Christ, its members he claimed,
And gave to them all care.

If ever an angel did walk this earth,
Then surely he was one,
For his words spoke of Heaven,
Of the Father, and of the Son.

Treated with disdain and disregard for his dignity,
"It matters not what befalls this shell,"
He said with humble humility,
"For when it dies, in Heaven, I will dwell."

One frozen night, wrapped in tattered cloth,
Laid bare to unforgiving cold,
He offered up a single prayer,
His eyes closed and he was home.

Joy

The true meaning of joy...
The answer I thought I knew,
But it was pointed out to me,
That I didn't have a clue.

Christ is the originator,
We must love Him above all else,
He says we must love each other,
As we love ourselves.

For the J stands for Jesus,
The almighty Son of God.
The O stands for the others,
That travel the same paths we trod.
The Y stands for yourself,
Usually the hardest of the three,
But the Lord says if we love not ourselves,
Then we love imperfectly.

Joy is not just an emotion,
That describes a state of mind,
And once we fully understand,
God's perfect love we'll find.
Joy crosses all human barriers,
And brings a people together.
Jews and Christians grafted as one,
Become the Lord's Olive tree forever.

I'll never take for granted,

Or forget the lesson learned,
When a man of God changed my life,
With that one simply stated word.

Christ Calls

Let me take this opportunity to witness for the Lord.
The Holy Ghost my armor, and the Word of God my sword.
No enemy can stand before me, Christ is my shield.
I strive to stand for righteousness, to sin I will not yield.

When temptation comes to call I'll cling to the cross.
With Christ as my strength I'll show that Devil who is boss.
I'm an heiress to the kingdom, the greatest ever known.
I claim power and authority because Christ is my own.

By His blood I have salvation, by His grace He calls me home.
I'll dwell in a place of safety, while Satan reaps what he has sown.
Christ will come forth in judgment on that predestined time and date.
An angel will wrap Satan in chains and cast him to his fate.

In the Lake of fire he will burn, but never will he die.
No escape, no second chance, in torment he will cry.
Christ will take death and sin and place it underneath His feet.
And the saints of all the ages in Paradise will meet.

As one body before the Lord with His Spirit we'll unite,
To live forever in that city that promises no night.
There will be no sickness there, and no more tears to cry.
All will be set right again in the by and by.

God is no respecter of persons, we can all claim victory.
Repent and claim your salvation before Him on your knees.
There is no greater love than what He has for you.
No greater strength that will help to see you through.

Armour

No greater power to put Satan in his lowly place.
No other God can save you by His grace.
He is gathering all His people, and drawing His children to His side.
One day soon, Heaven we'll see, and with Him there abide.

What He has given me, He freely gives to all.
Just listen for His voice and heed His lovely call.
There's a battle that is brewing between Heaven and Hell.
Put on your armor, pick up your sword, so that you can do well.

If you are not of Him against you He will come.
Soon you will have no time, for now, you have some.
Take advantage of His mercy, take advantage of today.
He promises no tomorrow so please don't delay.

It's not His will that we should perish, but have everlasting life.
The only way to Heaven is by the blood of Jesus Christ.
He can be your greatest friend or the worst of enemies.
So again I beg of you, find salvation on your knees.

You can call me a Holy roller or a religious freak,
But it is of the kingdom of Heaven that I now before you speak.
God is righteous in His judgment, and holy above all.
Open up your spiritual ears so Satan cannot cause your fall.

Accept Christ now, while time still remains,
And from all sin and unrighteousness refrain.
Stand upright and acceptable before the Lord I pray.
So you can hear, well done my child, on the fateful Judgment Day.

Daily Toil

I seek your will both night and day.
Though the path is hidden from my face.
Lord strengthen my waning faith.
Oh God, cover me with your grace.

Walk by faith when you can't see.
I promised I would always be,
By your side to strengthen thee.
Oh, child, you belong to me.

At every turn the children fight.
The bills pile up because money's tight.
The tunnels dark like I've lost my sight.
Oh, God, bathe me in your light.

Walk by faith when you can't see.
I promised I would always be,
By your side to strengthen thee.
Oh, child, you belong to me.

I am weak, Lord, but you are strong.
I fear I'm doing something wrong.
Place in my heart a brand new song.
Oh, God, keep me right where I belong.

Walk by faith when you can't see.
I promised I would always be,
By your side to strengthen thee.
Oh, child, you belong to me.

I know it's wrong to despair,
But life sometimes just isn't fair.
Right now it's more than I can bear.
Oh, God, I give to you my cares.

No matter where you are, I see.
For I'm in you and you're in me.
Trust in my truth, it'll set you free.
Oh, child, you belong to me.

Remember

As the children of God, we know this age doth end,
We wait with eager hearts for the reign of Christ to begin.
Our joy, however, is balanced by souls yet saved,
Because of faith never found, or lost along the way.
The evil in this world is known, and it multiplies,
Claiming those souls more precious than lives.
We see the sick give into death, and die in their beds,
Without once seeking God, or bowing their heads.
And those who've yet to perish, but are lost in their sin,
What, I pray, is to become of them?

When the rapture takes place, and they find they are alone,
I cannot fathom what fear and terror they will know.
Seven years of tribulation will be their penance and test,
Full heartache, and sickness, sadness, and death.
The battle now brewing between Heaven and Hell,
Will descend onto Earth, and in chaos dwell.
Family will mean nothing, and friends will mean less,
When survival and self-interest become one's sole focus.
They, for the second coming of Christ will pray,
When Satan becomes ruler of the day.

Do not set yourself upon a pedestal of pride,
For we are the commissioned army of Christ.
Every soul lost is one that we failed,
An enemy of God that we did not quell.
A tear that we caused to fall from the eyes,
Of the one we've sworn both our spirit and lives

By all means be full of joy, for we are the victorious,
But let us not forget to do as the Father first implored us.
We are the light in the darkness, the example they see,
So as you go forth remember, to Christ-like, be.

I'm Sending Out This Letter

Lord, I'm sending out this letter in hope of reaching you.
You said just to call out, but I'm having trouble getting through.
My life isn't full of heartache, You'll find no sickness here,
But although I cannot tell you why, I feel swallowed up in fear.
I go to church each Sunday, I pray morning, noon, and night.
Lord, I'm afraid I'm losing, this battle I'm trying to fight.
You said knock, and you would answer, seek, and I would find.
My spiritual hands are busted, and my throat is sore from crying.
I've done all that you've asked, I've walked through every door,
But nothing seems to satisfy, Lord, I desire more.

I'm sending out this letter, child, intent on reaching you.
Every time you've called out your prayers have gotten through.
I've protected you from heartache, and told sickness to stay away.
That spirit of fear is not of me, so just rebuke it in my Holy name.
I see you in my house each Sunday. Your prayers bring me delight.
When you feel weak from battle, remember you've won the fight.
I said knock and I would answer, and I've done so every time.
Never once have you searched for me when I wasn't there to find.
You've done all that I've asked, and walked through every door.
I see the hidden parts of you, and I know you desire more.

The treasures of Heaven are open. All I have, I freely give to you.
Hold fast to what you know child, for my coming will be soon.
I will gladly draw you unto me, and keep you safe by my side.
And I will be your reigning King, and with me you'll reside.
May you find rest in my arms, and your strength draw from me.
For it has always been my desire, to be everything you need.

When you're having trouble feeling like you're not getting through,
Remember that I came to earth, and found a cross to die for you.
And even when I'm silent, I'm still always standing close by.
For never let there be a doubt, you are forever, completely, mine.

Opportunity Knocks

I was walking down aisle seven at my local grocery store,
Thinking hmm, pork or chicken, which do I want more?
I'm distracted by a little girl who asks a simple question,
"Mama, we believe in God, does that make us Christian?"

I smiled at such innocence from the mouth of so sweet a babe,
As the mother stood perplexed, at a loss for what to say.
With boldness, I took the opportunity to witness for the Lord,
The Holy Ghost my armor, The word of God my sword.

The mother said not a word as I knelt before her child,
She merely nodded in gratitude and then smiled.
I said, "Little one, God would have you know,
He is everywhere you are, and everywhere you go.

He stays with you to protect you, His love for you great,
And when you call His name, He finds reason to celebrate.
Always believe in God for He believes in you,
And when things go hard, He will see you through.

Do not doubt you are a Christian, To Him, you belong.
Hold fast to your faith, sweet child, be strong."
My reward was twofold when I saw the mother's tearful nod,
I said to her, "You, as well, are a beloved of God."

As I returned to the business of my simple day to day,
I offered up to the Lord my sincerest praise.
I prayed He would tend the seeds, He'd allowed me to sow,
And that when came time to harvest, they would be carried home.

Look Up All His People

(song)

When the Spirit cries out for peace, but war is all that it receives...
Then look up. Oh, look up.

As Israel fights to stand, and we know that they are in His hands...
Then look up. Oh, look up.

Look up all His people. Keep your eyes on the east.
Listen for the angel's declaration. Watch for the King of Peace.
When we hear the trumpet blowing, then look for His return.
He promised us a place of safety before this world burns.

When sin grows day by day, and all that we can do is pray...
Then look up. Oh, look up.

When we can turn on our T.V. and watch fulfillment of prophecy...
Then look up. Oh, look up.

Look up all His people. Keep your eyes on the east.
Listen for the angel's declaration. Watch for the King of Peace.
When we hear the trumpet blowing, then look for His return.
He promised us a place of safety before this world burns.

The Day Our Savior Died

A crown of thorns an a pierced side,
Upon the cross our Savior dies,
His back torn from their mighty whips,
Down His body the blood now drips,
They lay Him in a tomb, and I turn away,
Lord of lords, our Savior died today,

Behind closed doors my grief I keep,
Lest my life they early reap,
Traitors marked, those who believe,
That Christ was Heaven's King,
How are we supposed to go on?
Three days He's now been dead and gone.

Behold what glory mine eyes now see!
My Savior stands before me.
He has risen from the grave complete,
With scars on His hands and feet,
I fall to the ground and cover my face,
"Lord, I was there when the stone was placed."

Confounded, I cannot my question quell,
"How is it you stand before me alive and well?"
My joy is o'er flowing as hope itself renews,
In His radiant presence, my fears are quickly soothed.
With a voice like many waters, He powerfully replies,
"For you to live eternally, first I had to die."

"Take my hand," He said, "and I'll show you the way,

Through trial and tribulation, I will keep you safe.
By my blood are you forgiven, and from sin set free.
By my death and resurrection you gain immortality.
My Father calls me home but another will soon come.
The Spirit of my Father, will dwell, until this age is done."

Emboldened by His promise I went forth to proclaim,
The Word of Jesus Christ. Glory to His name!
To be absent from the body is to be present with the Lord.
I'll shout it from the rooftops and knock on every door.
My fear has been removed, from no enemy will I turn,
For Christ has gone before me, and it's for His praise I yearn.

Let the Holy Ghost Come Down

(song)

Let the Holy Ghost come down in this place.
Let the Abba Father show His face.
Let there be no sight of sin.
Let the blood of Christ come in.
Let the Holy Ghost come down in this place.

Let the flesh here be weakened and the spirit overflow.
Let the will of God be spoken, so the heart can test and know,
That the Master is preparing, and it's almost time to go.
Time to reap of the Harvest that in love has been sown.
Let the Holy Ghost come down in this place.

May your preachers be anointed and your prophets prophesy.
May the flesh pass forever and the spirit come alive.
With our arms stretched toward Heaven, and our eyes upon the East.
We search for your coming, and the long awaited peace.
Let the Holy Ghost come down in this place.

May your bride kneel before you all clothed in spotless white.
Reflecting all your glory in a city with no night.
With the saints from all the ages singing destiny's new song.
Eternity before them dwelling right where they belong.
Let the Holy Ghost be forever in this place.

Let the Holy Ghost be forever in this place.
Let the Abba Father show His face.

Let there be no sight of sin.
Let the blood of Christ come in.
Let the Holy Ghost be forever in this place.

No One Like My Lord

(song)

No, there is no one like my Lord.
No, No,
No, there is no one like my Lord.

When I needed somebody to keep me in line,
He came as my Father just in time.

No, there is no one like my Lord.
No, No,
No, there is no one like my Lord.

When I needed a Savior because I was lost,
Here came Jesus up on the cross.

No, there is no one like my Lord.
No, No,
No, there is no one like my Lord.

When I needed some comfort, when I needed some hope,
Low and behold here came the Holy Ghost.

No, there is no one like my Lord.
No, No,
No, there is no one like my Lord.

All in one body, He is all three.
My Blessed Savior's everything to me.

No, there is no one like my Lord.

*No, No.
No, there is no one like my Lord.*

*There is no one like my Lord.
He's everything to me.*

Sunday Christians

(song)

Sunday Christians, where will you be,
If Jesus comes back on a Monday?

Will He say welcome, child,
Or you're one I do not know?
Will you be found acceptable,
Or is your walk just for show?
Will He find that you are praying?
Will He find you on your knees?
Or will He find you lacking,
Your spiritual man in need?

Oh, Sunday Christians, where will you be?

Sunday Christians, where will you be,
If Jesus comes back on a Wednesday?

Will He find you in a place,
That He is welcome in?
Or will He find you surrounded,
In a pit full of sin?
You can't serve Him just on Sunday,
For the weekdays come around,
And without His spirit in you,
You'll wind up on the ground.

Oh, Sunday Christians, where will you be?

When you think that you are sneaking by,
Your sins are bright as day.
You can't hide from the Lord,
For He knows you by name.
He sees the secrets of your heart,
He knows your end and where you start,
So take a stand and make a choice,
Lift up your hands and lift your voice.

Oh, Sunday Christians, know where you will be.

Upon a Hill

(song)

Many, many, years ago,
Upon a hill called Calvary,
My Savior took a walk alone,
And there He died for me.

My sins are covered by His blood,
What was lost is now found,
Thank you Father for the Son,
And my planted feet on solid ground.

He came from Heaven down to earth,
Through a Holy virgin birth,
Then He went to an early grave,
Rose again on that third day,
Said, some day, I'm coming back,
My word is true and.... It's a fact.

He took the stripes I could not bear,
So my body could be whole,
He showed how much He really cared,
Just in case I didn't know.

Now I serve Him night and day,
In search of Heaven's pearly gates,
Oh, Lord, I'll meet you there,
Where, with open arms, you await.

Liars Made

In time, they say, the pain will fade,
But they've themselves liars made,
For no such balm have I found,
Since first you slept beneath the ground.

I fear your death has sorrow cast,
And in its shadow grief doth last,
For when each dawn breaks anew,
So does the loss of losing you.

Dearly Departed

If you were here with us today,
It would be one full of joy and laughter.
We would sing happy birthday, Mom,
And may you have many more here after.
We would sit and talk about good old days,
That have somehow gone on by,
But standing here looking down at you,
We hold one another and cry.
For we stand in front of your grave, Mom,
And realize how much time has passed,
And we are forced to try and accept the fact,
That all good times don't last.
Your memory washes over us,
As clear as the day we said goodbye.
God chose to take home,
We don't pretend to understand why.
Instead we grieve for our loss,
While we rejoice in your victory,
For your salvation was assured,
On the cross at Calvary.
Today you turn two in Heaven.
We no longer count your years here.
We've come to honor your memory,
One we cherish and keep near.
Though we know you cannot see,
Your family is gathered as one.

*And you are missed most deeply,
By your mother, sister, daughter, and sons.*

As Her Mother

As her mother you remember:
The day of her birth.
Her invaluable worth.
The first words she said.
The first tears she shed.

As her mother you remember:
School the first day.
Her first friend made.
The fears she couldn't shake.
And her first big mistake.

As her mother you remember:
When she began her own life.
When she became someone's wife.
When her children came along.
When trials made her strong.

As her mother you remember:
When she grew too tired to stand.
When she reached for God's holy hand.
When salvation was given by grace.
When she at last finished the race.

As her mother you can no longer see:
But God has dried her last tear.
Conquered all her fears.
Holds her in the palm of His hand.
Until you can join her in the Promised Land.

Where the World Ends

I have been where the world ends,
Where the ocean kisses the sky,
Where the dolphins play in dancing waves,
And the seagulls swoop and dive.
Where pale pinks and purple hues,
Lazily along the horizon lay,
Until divine shades of perfect blues,
Signals the dawning of a new day.

The Ocean Rolls

Rolling shades of blues and greys,
White capped waves break over.
From the sun comes spearing rays,
Till the surface shimmers like glass.
A salty breeze caresses the land,
As ships head towards the harbor.
A storm is brewing by God's own hand.
We stand still while the ocean rolls.

Conclusion

*Admission.... Repentance....
Salvation.... Commission....
And Witness....
These are not mere words. They are keys.
They are the truths that reveal our belief.*

www.ingramcontent.com/pod-product-compliance
Lightning Source LLC
Chambersburg PA
CBHW021136300426
44113CB00006B/451